AN ATHEIST MANIFESTO

BY

JOSEPH LEWIS

THE FREETHOUGHT PRESS
ASSOCIATION: NEW YORK

COPYRIGHTED, 1954, AND IN THE
178TH YEAR OF AMERICAN
INDEPENDENCE BY JOSEPH LEWIS

All rights reserved

Second Edition, 1956 Third Edition, 1958

PRINTED IN THE UNITED STATES OF
AMERICA

JOSEPH LEWIS

Author of

THE TYRANNY OF GOD THE BIBLE UNMASKED VOLTAIRE: THE INCOMPARABLE INFIDEL SPAIN: A LAND BLIGHTED BY RELIGION BURBANK THE INFIDEL ATHEISM THE BIBLE AND THE PUBLIC SCHOOLS FRANKLIN THE FREETHINKER LINCOLN THE FREETHINKER MEXICO AND THE CATHOLIC CHURCH SOVIET RUSSIA AND THE CATHOLIC CHURCH SHALL CHILDREN RECEIVE RELIGIOUS INSTRUCTION? THE TEN COMMANDMENTS THOMAS PAINE: AUTHOR OF THE DECLARATION OF INDEPENDENCE IN THE NAME OF HUMANITY THE TRAGIC PATRIOT INSPIRATION AND WISDOM FROM THE WRITINGS OF THOMAS PAINE AN ATHEIST MANIFESTO INGERSOLL THE MAGNIFICENT

AN ATHEIST MANIFESTO

Many ask what difference does it make whether man believes in a God or not.

It makes a big difference.

It makes all the difference in the world.

It is the difference between being right and being wrong; it is the difference between truth and surmises--facts or delusion.

It is the difference between the earth being flat, and the earth being round.

It is the difference between the earth being the center of the universe, or a tiny speck in this vast and uncharted sea of multitudinous suns and galaxies.

It is the difference in the proper concept of life, or conclusions based upon illusion.

It is the difference between verified knowledge and the faith of religion.

It is a question of Progress or the Dark Ages.

The history of man proves that religion perverts man's concept of life and the universe, and has made him a cringing coward before the blind forces of nature.

If you believe that there is a God; that man was "created"; that he was forbidden to eat of the fruit of the "tree of knowledge"; that he disobeyed; that he is a "fallen angel"; that he is paying the penalty for his "sins," then you devote your time praying to appease an angry and jealous God.

If, on the other hand, you believe that the universe is a great mystery; that man is the product of evolution; that he is born without knowledge; that intelligence comes from experience, then you devote your time and energies to improving his condition with the hope of securing a little happiness here for yourself and your fellow man.

That is the difference.

If man was "created," then someone made a grievous mistake.

It is inconceivable that any form of intelligence would waste so much time and effort to make such an inferior piece of life-- with all the "ills that flesh is heir to," and with all the misery and suffering that is so essential a part of living.

If man is a "fallen angel," by the commission of a "sin," then disease and sorrow are part of God's inscrutable plan as a penalty imposed upon him for his "disobedience," and man's entire life is devoted to the expiation of that sin so as to soften the indictment before the "Throne of God."

Man's atonement consists in making himself as miserable as possible by praying, fasting, masochism, flagellations and other forms of torture.

This sadistic delusion causes him to insist that others--under pain of punishment--be as miserable as himself, for fear that if others fail to do as he does, it will provoke the wrath of his tyrant God to a more severe chastisement.

The inevitable result is that Man devotes his life, not to the essentials of living and the making of a happy home, but to the building of temples and churches where he can "lift his voice to God" in a frenzy of fanaticism, and eventually he becomes a victim of hysteria.

His time and energy are wasted to cleanse

his "soul," which he does not possess, and to save himself from a future punishment in hell which exists only in his imagination.

Religious hallucinations take on many forms.

Some do not wash themselves; some wash only their fingers; some think that the filthier they are, the "holier" they are; some cut off their hair, while others let it grow long; some refuse to stand up, while others refuse to sit down; some amputate their genitals, and some their breasts; some pull out their teeth, and others wither their limbs; some fast, and others gorge themselves; some cover their heads with sand, and others with sackcloth and ashes; some talk continuously, and others remain silent; some are celibates, and others are profligates; some stand on their heads; some brand themselves, while others pierce their nose, eyes and ears.

Nuns cut off their hair to make themselves as unsightly as possible--to make themselves repulsive to the opposite sex; there are monks who have vowed never to look upon the face of a woman, and Franciscans still wear ropes around their bodies as a symbol of flagellation.

There is hardly a form of insanity or delusion that has not been induced by some sort of religious belief.

To laugh on the "Sabbath," at one time, was considered the sin of sins.

How rightfully Robert G. Ingersoll said that, "Christianity has made more lunatics than it ever provided asylums for."

On the other hand, we do not believe that Man is a depraved human being. We do not believe that there is a tyrant God, or that there is a hell, and that man will suffer the pains and penalties of eternal torment. We do not believe that you should make yourself as miserable as possible Here in the hope of securing some happiness "Hereafter."

We do not believe that disease is a punishment for sin.

We believe that disease is a natural consequence of the processes of life, and that the "ills of the flesh" inevitably follow where one form of life lives upon another, and where "at the banquet of life each in turn is a guest and a dish."

It is only by understanding the nature of disease that man has been able, even in a small degree, to protect himself from the ravages of its destruction.

The use of prayer to cure disease has been responsible for epidemics that have, on many occasions, almost wiped out the human race. Prayer has had no more effect upon disease than it has upon health. It merely permits the disease to continue its course and increase the suffering of the victim.

If priests--of all clans--were free of disease and immune to death, then there might be some basis for the claim of the religionists. But these "men of God" are victims of the natural course of life, "even as you and I." They enjoy no exemptions. They suffer the same ills; they feel the same sensations; they are subject to the same passions of the body, the same frailties of the mind, are victims of circumstances and misfortune, and they meet inevitable death just as every other person. They commit the same kind of crimes as other mortals, and especially, because of their "calling," many are notoriously involved in the embezzlement of church funds. Nor does their calling protect them from the "passions of the flesh." The scandalous conduct of many "men of the cloth," in the realm of moral turpitude, often ends in murder. That is why there are so many "men of God" in our jails, and why so many have paid the supreme penalty in the death chair.

They are not free from a single rule of life; what others must endure, they likewise must experience. They cannot protect themselves from the forces of nature, and the laws of life, any more than you can. What they can do, you can do, too. Their claims of being "anointed" and "vicars of God" on earth are false and hypocritical.

If they cannot fulfill their promises while you are alive, how can they accomplish them when you are dead?

If they are impotent Here, where they could demonstrate their powers, how ridiculous are their promises to accomplish them in the "Hereafter," the mythical abode which exists only in their dishonest or deluded imagination?

The illusions of life are many and varied.

Things are not always what they seem to be,

and it is well known that "appearances are deceiving."

That is why it is so difficult for some people to understand the nature of disease, and why it has taken man so long to comprehend the true conditions of life.

This deception prevails in matters of great importance, as well as in matters of little consequence.

There is no "voice of nature" to tell man that which is true and that which is false, nor to warn him of the dangers of life. He must find the truth for himself, and only after very bitter experiences.

The first piece of deception of man, after his so-called mental awakening, was his inability to conceive of any scheme of life except from his own primitive concept of limited intelligence.

He could not conceive the earth and the universe except as being "created," and from his own feeling of revenge, he could not conceive of the suffering of life except as a punishment for some "disobedience." Primitive though he be, he did not inflict pain and punishment upon the innocent.

This diabolical scheme could only come from a "merciful" God.

As an illustration of this concept of primitive man in this respect is the delusion he experiences when he believes that the sun "rises and sets," when as a matter of fact, it is the sun which is "stationary" as far as the earth is concerned, and it is the earth that "moves," as Galileo so courageously maintained--at the cost of his liberty.

There is a delusion that the sun shines and the water falls from the clouds to make the flowers bloom.

To the religionist this is an indication of the "beauty" in nature.

It is nothing of the kind.

Poisonous plants and obnoxious weeds are equally nourished by the warmth of the sun and the moisture of the water.

Is this, then, an indication of the "ugliness" of nature?

Certainly not.

Both are inevitable consequences of the

environment in which they live. It could not be otherwise.

Is the hippopotamus one of nature's masterpieces?

Is its face and form the perfection of beauty and grace?

Would you consider this animal a work of living art if you were responsible for it?

And yet, if this beast could talk, it would probably say that its environment was made for its benefit and that its marvelous features, particularly its mouth, was especially "designed" for its enjoyment, and that its whole body was made in the "image and likeness of God."

The fact that the hippopotamus has survived these millions of years of the evolutionary process and still thrives today is proof that it is equally as favored by Nature as is man.

To nature the blossoms of the flowers and the obnoxious weeds are identical, and the fragrance of the one and the stench of the other are equally alike; both, if they could talk, would boast of Nature's preference for them.

While, as a matter of fact, both would be wrong.

The sun does not shine to bring us its necessary light and warmth without also bringing to light some new burden for our overtroubled hearts to bear; and everything in the universe shares the same and inevitable consequences.

While it is true that it is "an ill wind that blows no good," it is also true that what is "one man's meat is another man's poison."

To Nature matters of "great importance" and matters of "little consequence" are on an equal basis. The one is not "favored" above the other. It is the survival of the fittest, and not the most desirable that survives.

When conditions are favorable to the "wild" animals, they thrive by killing the other forms of life upon which they live, and when conditions are favorable to man, he kills and lives upon the forms of life which he considers exist solely for his pleasure and benefit.

To nature the germs of disease, as a form of life, are equally as important as the other forms of life that "breathe and have their being."

When conditions are favorable to the virus of influenza and pneumonia, we have what is known as an epidemic, and when conditions are favorable to the growth of cancer, it has what we might term a "Roman Holiday" by destroying a third of our population.

Germs of disease are merely invisible wild animals.

They are forms of life that thrive upon the soil of the human body.

Prayer has about as much effect upon them as it would have upon the hungry tiger ready to devour you.

A bullet from a gun would be far more effective against the tiger, and knowledge of the nature of the germs of disease, and the discovery of the methods of destroying them, are comparable to the invention of the gun and its use against the ferocious animal.

The knowledge of the one protects you against the invisible enemies of destruction, while the invention of the gun protects you against being destroyed by the wild beasts.

The germs of disease and the hungry tiger are both determined upon the same objective--your destruction--one by eating you in "chunks" and the other by minutely gnawing you away "piecemeal."

The results are identical.

It is not necessary to moralize upon the difference.

But this we know, that in our present scheme of life, as Ingersoll so eloquently states, "The hands that help are better far than lips that pray."

Our bodies are as much "meat" for the disease germs that eat us as the animal that furnishes the meat for our appetites.

Or as Shakespeare puts it:

"... in the sweetest bud The eating canker dwells."

In a broader and more comprehensive concept of disease, Shakespeare says, it is, as if a

"God omnipotent Is mustering in his clouds... Armies of pestilence; and they shall strike Your children yet unborn and unbegot...."

Who are you to say which one is the more favored in this scheme of life--the germs of disease or man--which one is preferred by nature; which one is more important than the other, since the ends accomplished are the same?

The life of the disease germ came into existence by the same process as did the life of man.

It is just as much a part of nature as is the dimpled babe.

If we cannot live without sunshine and water, neither can the germs of disease.

It might well be that we are nothing more than "disease germs" in the environment in which we live. The same basic construction by which they live forms the same pattern upon which our life is built.

To nature the night is just as important as the day, and the life of the germ we call disease is as important as the life of the body upon which it feeds.

It follows the same law of life; it is born, reproduces and dies.

There are forms of life that live by night that are equally as favored by nature as those which live by day.

Freaks of all kinds exist in nature--from the utterly ridiculous to the terrifying monstrosities. This is proof of the lack of design in Nature as far as man is concerned.

When man comes to the realization that he is not the "favorite" of God; that he was not specially created, that the universe was not made for his benefit, and that he is subject to the same laws of nature as all other forms of life, then, and not until then, will he understand that he must rely upon himself, and himself alone, for whatever benefits he is to enjoy; and devote his time and energies to helping himself and his fellow men to meet the exigencies of life and to set about to solve the difficult and intricate problems of living.

The recognition of a problem is the first step to its solution--

We are not "fallen" angels, nor were we "created" perfect.

On the contrary, we are the product of millions of years of an unpurposed evolution.

We are the descendants and inheritors of all the defects of our primitive ancestry--the evolution of the myriad forms of life from the infinitesimal to the mammoth--from the worm to the dinosaur.

The most important step in the development of man is the recognition of the fact that we are born without knowledge, and that the acquisition of knowledge is a slow and painful process.

If all man needed upon earth was a "knowledge of God," then why the necessity of establishing educational institutions?

Unless a child is taught to talk, it will never be able to speak the language of our tongue. Without teaching the child the rudiments of speech, he would be unable to communicate his thoughts to others. Without proper training his "grunts" of expression would be meaningless, and the only way he could express himself would be by the primitive instinct of making signs and by pointing.

The brain needs the same kind of training as

any other part of the body that requires exercise for development. Nourishment for the mind is just as necessary as nourishment for the body.

Just as there are some foods which have been so adulterated and refined that when eaten they add no nourishment to the body, so there are truths which have been adulterated by religion and superstition so as to be utterly valueless in nourishing the mind with intelligence.

Education becomes the primary object of civilization.

As Thomas Paine says: "Wisdom is not the purchase of a day."

The church knows that an educated man is an unbeliever.

That is why there is a continual struggle on the part of the clergy to adulterate education with superstition. To maintain their untenable position they must keep the people shackled to a form of mental slavery.

Both fear and superstition are forms of a contagious disease.

The ignorance of man produced natural fears of the elements of nature. What he could not understand he attributed to malevolent spirits whose primary purpose was to punish and harm him. Under this spell it seems almost incredible that he ever advanced from his state of primitive ignorance.

His fears produced such fantastic monsters of the air that it was first necessary to relieve his tormented mind of these terrifying myths of ghosts and gods before he was able to acquire even the simplest rudiments of knowledge.

Man's ignorance and fears made him an easy prey of priests.

His gullibility was such that he believed everything he was told.

He soon became a slave to these liars and hypocrites.

And what did the priests tell him?

They told him that God had made a special revelation in a book called the Bible, and that it was necessary to believe every word in that book in order that he might save his soul. They told him that if he disobeyed their commands, he would suffer eternal damnation in a hell where "the fire never ceases, and where the worm never dies."

They also told him that it was a sin for him to read that book, and that the priest was especially ordained by God to interpret the meaning of each and every word.

And what was the priest's interpretation of the text of that book?

It was that man was a corrupt and sinful being, and that in order to be saved from punishment after death, he had to give a substantial part of the fruits of his labor to the priest to pray for him, and intercede with God on his behalf, so as to mitigate the punishment to which he had already been doomed.

What a diabolical scheme of fraud by which to live upon the sweat and labor of others.

It was such a profitable scheme that the priests began to maintain their power by the force of arms.

As a result there came into existence the twin tyrannies of church and state.

It seems incredible that such nonsense was ever imposed upon suffering humanity, and nonsense it would be were it not so tragic.

So fearful did he become that he thought that he could not live without the "protection" of the priests, and as Ingersoll said, "as long as people wanted Popes, plenty of hypocrites will be found to take their place...."

Ingersoll further declared: "The priests pretended to stand between the wrath of the gods and the helplessness of man. He was man's attorney at the court of heaven. He carried to the invisible world a flag of truce, a protest and a request. He came back with a command, with authority and power. Man fell upon his knees before his own servant, and the priest, taking advantage of the awe inspired by his supposed influence with the gods, made of his fellow-man a cringing hypocrite and slave."

As long as there is one person suffering an injustice; as long as one person is forced to bear an unnecessary sorrow; as long as one person is subject to an undeserved pain, the worship of a God is a demoralizing humiliation.

As long as there is one mistake in the universe; as long as one wrong is permitted to exist; as long as there is hatred and antagonism among mankind, the existence of a God is a moral impossibility.

Ingersoll said: "Injustice upon earth renders the justice of heaven impossible."

Man's inhumanity to man will continue as long as man loves God more than he loves his fellow man.

The love of God means wasted love.

"For God and Country" means a divided allegiance--a 50 per cent patriot.

The most abused word in the language of man is the word "God."

The reason for this is that it is subject to so much abuse.

There is no other word in the human language that is as meaningless and incapable of explanation as is the word "God."

It is the beginning and end of nothing.

It is the Alpha and Omega of Ignorance.

It has as many meanings as there are minds. And as each person has an opinion of what the word God ought to mean, it is a word without premise, without foundation, and without substance.

It is without validity.

It is all things to all people, and is as meaningless as it is indefinable.

It is the most dangerous in the hands of the unscrupulous, and is the joker that trumps the ace.

It is the poisoned word that has paralyzed the brain of man.

"The fear of the Lord" is not the beginning of wisdom; on the contrary, it has made man a groveling slave; it has made raving lunatics of those who have attempted to interpret what God "is" and what is supposed to be our "duty" to God.

It has made man prostitute the most precious things of life--it has made him sacrifice wife, and child, and home.

"In the name of God" means in the name of nothing--it has caused man to be a wastrel with the precious elixir of life, because there is no God.

Ingersoll could not understand the mind of those who, once having been told the truth, preferred to remain under the spell of superstition and in ignorance. He could not understand why people would not accept "new truths with gladness."

He also knew, however, that once a person's mind had been poisoned with religious superstition, it was almost impossible to free it from the paralyzing fear which destroyed its ability to think.

It is now established by verifiable evidence that religion stultifies the brain and is the great obstacle in the path of intellectual progress.

The more religious a person is, the more he is steeped in ignorance and superstition, the less is his sense of moral responsibility. The more intelligent a person, the less religious he is. There is an old saying that "where there are three scientists, there are two atheists."

The countries whose governments are dominated by religion and religious institutions are the most backward. By the same token, the countries whose people are the most enlightened, and whose governments are based upon the principle of secularism--the separation of church and state--are the most progressive.

And let me tell you: When man is intellectually free, the progress he will make is beyond calculation.

What better illustration than this: More progress has been made since the Declaration of Independence and the American Revolution than was made in the previous five thousand years!

Yes, more intellectual and material progress has been made by man since the establishment of the American Republic than during all the intervening years from the Pharaohs of Egypt up to and including the time of "the grandeur that was Greece, and the glory that was Rome."

And there is a good and valid reason for this.

It was because "in 1776 our fathers retired the gods from politics." The basic principle of the American Republic is the freedom of man in society.

The Declaration of Independence was the product of Intellectual Emancipation, and that is why, from thenceforth, our date of existence should be recorded, not from the mythical birth of Jesus Christ, but from the day of our Independence!

This should be the year one hundred and seventy-eight in our calendar!

Despite discouraging signs here and there, the seeds of freedom planted by the American Revolution will take root, and throughout the world, if man will learn to zealously guard his freedom, Peace and Progress will come to all the world.

Could there be a more significant illustration than this:

Practically in our own lifetime, and certainly since the Declaration of Independence, man has wrought the most amazing achievements in the field of science and progress ever recorded in human history.

Not in their order, nor according to their significance, do I record the following:

Anesthesia was discovered.

Do you know what it means to relieve man of his pain and suffering? Anesthesia is the most humane of all of man's accomplishments, and what a merciful accomplishment it was.

For this great discovery we are indebted to Dr. W. T. G. Morton.

Do you know that the religionists opposed the use of anesthesia on the ground that God sent pain as a punishment for sin, and it was considered the greatest of sacrileges to use it--just think of it, a sin to relieve man of his misery! What a monstrous perversion! This one instance alone should convince you of the difference in believing in God or not.

No believer in God would have spent his energies to discover anesthesia. He would have been in mortal fear of the wrath of his God for interfering with his "divine plan," of making man suffer for having eaten of the fruit of the "Tree of Knowledge."

The very crux of the matter is in this one instance.

Man seeks to relieve his fellow man from

the suffering of disease and the pangs of mental agony. The believers in God are content that man's suffering is ordained, and therefore he accepts life and its trials and tribulations as a penance for living.

The fear of the wrath of God has been a stumbling block to progress.

When Dr. James Young Simpson sought to apply anesthesia to a woman in childbirth, the clergymen of his day foamed at the mouth and spat upon him with vituperation and abuse, for attempting to violate God's direct command that "in pain thou shalt bring forth children," as based upon the idiotic text of the Bible. But Dr. Simpson persisted despite the ravings of the religious lunatics of his day.

The importance of Dr. Simpson's application of anesthesia to the relief of pain in childbirth, and his open defiance of the religionists, are beyond the measure of words to evaluate.

The X-ray was discovered in our time.

Professor Wilhelm Roentgen deserves our everlasting debt of gratitude for this contribution. Its application alone in the field of medicine makes it one of the greatest contributions to the service of man.

Dr. Karl Lansteiner's discovery of the composition of the blood--made in our time--has been responsible for the saving of countless thousands of lives.

Blood was also feared by the religionists, and a taboo was placed upon all those who touched it, as being contaminated.

Even the dissection of the human body was prohibited by religion.

The study of human anatomy is within our own time, and the fruitful results of this scientific exploring of man's physical structure are incalculable.

It is needless, I think, to tell you why the study of human body is so recent. Until the emancipation of the mind of man from the thraldom and shackles of religion, it was taught and believed as a "religious truth," and maintained under penalty of eternal damnation, that if the human body was dissected, God would not be able to recognize you on the day of resurrection!

Such has been the paralyzing menace of

religion that has prevailed over the mind of man.

The discovery of the chemistry of food and its application to nutrition has contributed more to the health of the human race than all the Gods, clergymen and priests since the dawn of existence.

Preventive medicine has accomplished amazing results in bringing health to, and prolonging, the life of the people.

Hygiene and its application have saved millions upon millions from disease and premature death. It has stayed the "hand of God" in his madness in spreading deaths from epidemics of disease.

Charles Darwin published his "Origin of Species" and the great principle of evolution was promulgated.

Modern emancipated medicine has reduced the infant death rate by more than 50 per cent, and has been responsible for more than doubling the life span of man within the past century.

Just think of it! All of this within our own lifetime!

All of this and more since the day of American independence!

And listen to these words of Dr. Paul D. White, founder of the American Heart Association. He said:

"Those of us doctors who graduated from medical school thirty to forty years ago, look back now at the almost unbelievable ignorance about heart disease that then existed. *More knowledge has come since then than had been acquired in all the centuries before.*" (Italics mine).

Man was taught in the past that the heart, like the voice, was the "gift of God," and it was too sacred for man to probe into its workings. What were the results? Millions died who could have been saved; millions lived as horrible cripples who could have lived a normal life if man in the past, had had the courage, that he has today, to seek relief from the terrors of disease.

Such is the amazing progress that has been made when man relies upon his own efforts to solve his problems, whether they concern his health, or his social or political affairs.

It was only within the past forty years that

Dr. James B. Herrick properly diagnosed the cause of coronary thrombosis from which followed the amazing progress that has since been attained in combating this greatest of killers.

I, for one, wish to place upon the brow of Dr. Herrick my laurel leaf of thanks for his great accomplishment in medicine.

What wonders have been accomplished since the invention of the steam engine, the automobile, radio, television, electronic devises, and the thousand and one other discoveries and inventions too numerous to mention.

The educational benefit of the motion picture will far outstrip its entertainment value, and its use in nearly every department of learning makes it one of man's most valuable inventions.

Think of Benjamin Franklin's discovery of the relationship of electricity and lightning and the condemnation heaped upon him for his defiance of "The Prince of the Power of the Air."

And of the Wright brothers, and the dire penalty they were to suffer for "flying into the face of God."

Lightning, once feared as the wrathful manifestation of an angry God, was reproduced in the laboratory by that electrical wizard and atheist, Charles P. Steinmetz.

The telephone, wireless telegraphy, the steam engine, refrigeration, the washing and sewing machines, the mechanical weaving of cloth, and the myriad uses of electric and atomic power will make man the master of his destiny once he frees himself from the myth of a tyrant God.

Ingersoll best expressed man's inventions and their uses when he said that, "Science took the thunderbolt from the gods, and in the electric spark, freedom, with thought, with intelligence and with love, sweeps under all the waves of the sea; science, free thought, took a tear from the cheek of unpaid labor, converted it into steam, and created the giant that turns, with tireless arms, the countless wheels of toil."

Deprive man of the use of his discoveries and inventions of the past century and he will think he has been returned to barbarism.

Look what Thomas A. Edison's invention of the electric light did for man--it lengthened his life, it gave more hours to the day, and increased his comforts beyond anything previously known or imagined, and added immeasurably to his joy of living.

Even Joshua's fictitious performance of stopping the sun and the moon fades into nothingness when compared with this sublime achievement.

Nor must we forget Edison's invention for reproducing the human voice--and please grant me a moment's indulgence to say that I had the great honor to know Thomas A. Edison, and Edison honored me by calling me his friend.

If printing has been hailed as one of the world's great inventions, what must we say of the phonograph? While printing preserves man's thoughts on paper, the phonograph preserves not only his thoughts but also his voice!

The song of the skylark is no longer "wasted upon the desert air."

Thomas A. Edison--the greatest of human benefactors--wrested from nature her most guarded secret--the mystery of the human voice.

He disproved, as it was once believed, that the human voice, like the heart, was the "gift of God." He demonstrated that the human voice was merely the natural mechanism of sound produced by air of the lungs passing over the "cords" of the throat and larynx in the same manner as are sounds produced by the strings of a musical instrument.

As a result of Edison's invention, man himself has already produced artificially every manifestation of the human voice!

If the voice was part of "God's plan," how do we account for its absence in the giraffe? This animal has no larynx and therefore no vocal cords, and as a consequence it cannot talk or make sounds with its throat!

The giraffe is proof of the lack of design in nature and the blindness of the forces of evolutionary life.

To list all the great discoveries in the field of science and medicine during the past century, such as aspirin, insulin, penicillin, and the streptomycin drugs would require the undivided attention of a medical historian and a veritable encyclopedia to record them.

And yet, there are still many diseases that plague man of which he has no knowledge. They eat and ravage his mind and body with excruciating pain and torture, and he is utterly helpless against them. He not only does not know their origin, but has not the slightest inkling of their nature or how to fortify himself against their attacks. He must sit, like a condemned criminal, in agonizing torture, waiting for blessed death.

If man, and the other forms of life upon this earth, are a mere by-product of an "over-all plan" of a "supreme intelligence," then I denounce such a scheme as tyrannical and barbaric.

Why should we be made to suffer such excruciating pains and penalties of life to satisfy that from which we derive no benefit, and where death negates all of our efforts; and which makes the purpose of life, our hopes and desires, our ambitions and aspirations, a cruel mockery?

O prayer, thy name is failure!

O God, thou art a cruel myth!

You will not find a single mention of these great humanitarian achievements in the so-called "Book of Books"; not a single reference about the nature and cure of disease; not a word regarding those inventions that have so mercifully lifted the burden of toil from the backs of labor.

And there is good reason for it.

The Biblical writers not only had no knowledge of these things, but they had a perverted concept of life and the universe. Their concept was that man was a victim of blood pollution and his only salvation was by a blood atonement.

I remember once seeing a small pamphlet entitled, "What the Bible Teaches about Morality." On opening the little booklet, it was discovered to be nothing but blank pages! Another such pamphlet might very appropriately be published entitled, "What the Bible Reveals about Disease, Medicine and Health," and blank pages should be used for all the Bible contains about these vital subjects.

On the contrary, these benefits have been denounced by the believers in the Bible, and by the representatives of the Bible's deity as being contrary to "God's Plan."

Does not the Bible plainly state that only by the sweat of his brow is man to labor for the bread he eats?

Here is the exact Biblical quotation: "In the sweat of thy face thou shalt eat bread..." and why? Only because he sought knowledge.

And does not the Bible God place a curse upon man for the knowledge that has been such a solace and benefit to him?

Here is another exact Biblical quotation: "...cursed be the ground for thy sake; in pain thou shalt eat of it all the days of thy life."

The Bible is a lie. It is a fake and a fraud.

I denounce this book and its God.

I hold it in utter detestation.

Every man and woman who has contributed to the relief of the pain and suffering of humanity has been an infidel to the Bible God!

Every new invention, every new discovery

for the benefit of man violates these Biblical edicts!

I say, seek knowledge--defy this tyrant God--it is your only salvation.

It is because of the Biblical curse on man's search for knowledge, which has so paralyzed his mind during the past ages, and its detrimental effect upon progress, that makes the Bible the most wicked, the most detestable, the most pernicious, and the most obnoxious book ever published.

It has been a curse to the human race.

It is the duty of every brave and honest man and woman to do everything in his and her power to destroy the influence of this utterly stupid and vicious book, with its infantile concept of life and its nonsense concerning the universe.

It is their duty to do everything within their power to stop its demoralizing and paralyzing influence upon the life of man.

We will never achieve intellectual liberty until the wickedness of this book has been discarded with the belief in the flatness of the earth.

If you do not want to stop the wheels of progress; if you do not want to go back to the Dark Ages; if you do not want to live again under tyranny, then you must guard your liberty, and you must not let the church get control of your government.

If you do, you will lose the greatest legacy ever bequeathed to the human race-- intellectual freedom.

Now let me tell you another thing.

If all the energy and wealth wasted upon religion--in all of its varied forms--had been spent to understand life and its problems, we would today be living under conditions that would seem almost like Utopia.

Most of our social and domestic problems would have been solved, and equally as important, our understanding and relations with the other peoples of the world would have, by now, brought about universal peace.

Man would have a better understanding of his motives and actions, and would have learned to curb his primitive instincts for revenge and retaliation. He would, by now, know that wars of hate, aggression, and aggrandizement are only productive of more hate and more human suffering.

The enlightened and completely emancipated man from the fears of a God and the dogma of hate and revenge would make him a brother to his fellow man.

He would devote his energies to discoveries and inventions, which theology previously condemned as a defiance of God, but which have proved so beneficial to him.

He would no longer be a slave to a God and live in cringing fear!

To build a church when a school house is needed is to perpetrate a theft upon education.

To build a church when a hospital is needed is to take from the parched lips of the sick the cup of relief and from the suffering the merciful hand of help.

When the object of man's conduct will be to improve the conditions of his fellow man and not the appeasement of a mythical God, he will become more understanding and more indulgent of the frailties, mistakes, and action of others, and by the same token he will become more appreciative of their efforts.

He will develop a greater consciousness to avoid mistakes and to prevent injury. Life and its living will take on a greater significance, and our efforts and energies will be devoted to creating as much joy and happiness as possible for all living creatures.

Unless death is made a lesson for the living, the life lived is wasted.

Why should life come into existence only to be destroyed? One dies and another is born--for what? A few miserable hours of life--then oblivion!

With this recognition of the finality of death, no one should willingly withhold acts that would bring benefits, joy or happiness to others. In death, the hesitant act can no longer be performed--the word of praise is as impossible as yesterday's return.

What perversity justified inflicting pain, suffering and death upon others who have done no wrong?

If death ends all, why fight while we are living? Why shorten life with unnecessary pain and suffering?

How futile are the petty problems of individuals, with their hates and jealousies, when all vanish with death?

All the prayers in the world cannot wipe out one injustice.

Every wrong is irreparable.

The dead cannot forgive.

All the tears and sighs are of no avail.

Forgiveness cannot be granted when lips cannot move. Praise cannot be heard when ears cannot hear; joy cannot be experienced when the heart no longer beats; and the happiness of an affectionate embrace can no longer be felt when arms are limp and the eyes are forever closed.

You are to make up your mind whether it is to be God or man.

Whether you are to be free or a slave.

Whether it is to be progress or stagnation.

As long as man loves a phantom in the sky

more than he loves his fellow man, there will never be peace upon this earth; so long as man worships a Tyrant as the "Fatherhood of God," there will never be a "Brotherhood of Man."

You must make the choice, you must come to the decision.

Is it to be God or Man? Churches or Homes--preparation for death or happiness for the living?

If ever man needed an example of the benefit of the one against the other, he need but read the pages of history for proof of how religion retarded progress and provoked hatred among the children of men.

When theology ruled the world, man was a slave.

The people lived in huts and hovels.

They were clad in rags and skins; they devoured crusts and gnawed bones; the priests wore garments of silk and satin; carried mitres of gold and precious stones, robbed the poor and lived upon the fat of the land!

Here and there a brave man appeared to question their authority.

These martyrs to intellectual emancipation slowly and painfully broke the spell of superstition and ushered in the Age of Reason and the Dawn of Science.

Man became the only god that man can know.

He no longer fell upon his knees in fear.

He began to enjoy the fruits of his own labor.

He discovered a way to relieve himself from the drudgery of continuous toil; he began to enjoy a few comforts of life--and for the first time upon this earth he found a few moments for happiness.

It is far more important to learn how to live than to learn how to pray.

A new day and a new era dawned for him.

His labors produced enormous dividends.

He looked at the sky for the first time and saw that it was blue! He searched the heavens and found no God. He no longer feared the manifestations of nature.

The stars, however, are not the alphabet upon which to read the destiny of man.

We not only do not believe that man is punished for his "sins," but emphatically state that there is no such thing as sin.

There are wrongs and injustices, but no sin.

Sin, like purgatory and hell, was invented by priests, first to frighten, and then to rob the living.

We do not fear these myths and curses, and that is why we devote our time and energies to help our fellow man.

That is why we build educational institutions and seek, by a slow and painful process, to teach man the true nature of the universe and a proper understanding of his place as a member in society. At the same time we try to fortify his mind with courage to withstand the rebuffs, the trials and tribulations of life. That it is a difficult and arduous task no one can deny because we cannot correct all of "God's mistakes" in one life time.

As Ingersoll so succinctly states: "Nature cannot pardon."

Remember this: You are not a depraved human being.

You have no sins to atone for.

There is no need for fear.

There are no ghosts--holy or otherwise.

Stop making yourself miserable for "the love of God."

Drive this monster of tyrannic fear from your mind, and enjoy the inestimable freedom of an emancipated human being.

The only duty you owe is to yourself and to your family.

The duty you owe to yourself is to do the best you can, and the duty you owe to your family is to endeavor to make them happy.

Emancipate yourself from these stultifying creeds, and protect your children from the contamination of religion.

Get off your knees, stand erect, and look the

whole world in the face.

Get all the joy and happiness you can out of life.

Enjoy the fruits of your labor and waste it not upon the myth of heaven; support not the parasites of God.

Do not knowingly harm another human being; do not knowingly injure your fellow man.

All forms of life have feeling, do not make them suffer.

As Shakespeare says:

"The poor beetle, that we tread upon, In corporal sufferance finds a pang as great As when a giant dies."

Kindness is a magic solvent.

While we know that sometimes "ingratitude is more strong than traitor's arms," we also know that "mercy is twice blest; it blesses him that gives and him that takes," and, it should be remembered that while Loyalty is the most important of the virtues, Patience is the most valuable.

Become a courageous human being and do the best you can under any and all circumstances in this imperfect and troublesome world.

Be brave enough to live and be brave enough to die, knowing that when the Grim Reaper comes, you did the best you could and that the world is better for your having lived.

A God could do no more.

I will stand between you and the hosts of heaven.

I am not afraid.

I will act as your attorney before the Bar of Judgment.

I will assume all responsibility.

My services are free.

Put the blame on me.

Break the chains of mental slavery to religious superstition.

Arise and become a free and independent

human being.

Dignify yourself as a Man, and justify your living by being a Brother to All Mankind and a Citizen of the Universe.

Made in the USA
San Bernardino, CA
16 June 2014